EARTH'S BIOMES

TUNDRA

TH'S BIOMES

TUNDRA

TOM WARHOL

 Marshall Cavendish
Benchmark
New York

To Heather for her research help, and Bob for his tireless interest and PR work!

Marshall Cavendish Benchmark
99 White Plains Road
Tarrytown, New York 10591-9001
www.marshallcavendish.us

Editor: Karen Ang
Editorial Director: Michelle Bisson
Art Director: Anahid Hamparian
Series Designer: Patrice Sheridan

Library of Congress Cataloging-in-Publication Data

Warhol, Tom.
Tundra / by Tom Warhol.
p. cm.—(Earth's biomes)
Summary: "Explores tundra biomes and covers where they are located as well
as the plants and animals that inhabit them"—Provided by publisher.
Includes bibliographical references and index.
ISBN-13: 978-0-7614-2193-1
ISBN-10: 0-7614-2193-9
1. Tundra ecology—Juvenile literature. 2. Tundras—Juvenile literature.
I. Title. II. Series.

QH541.5.T8W37 2007
577.5'86—dc22
2006015822

Front cover: A caribou on tundra below Mt. McKinley
Title page: Arctic tundra
Back cover: South American páramo
Photo research by Candlepants, Inc.
Cover Photo: Paul A. Souders / Corbis

The photographs in this book are used by permission and through the courtesy of:
Peter Arnold Inc: S.J. Krasemann, 3, 31; Ed Reschke, 14, 60; BIOS, 32. *Minden Pictures:* Michio Hoshino, 7, 22,
35; Matthias Breiter, 18; Winfried Wisniewski/Foto Natura, 36; Michio Hoshio, 37; Michael Quinton, 38; Jim
Brandenburg, 40; Carr Clifton, 43; Frans Lanting, 44; Tui De Roy, 46, 59, 64; Flip de Nooyer/Foto Natura, 48;
Pete Oxford, 56; Patricio Robles Gil/Sierra Madre, 68, 69. *Photo Researchers Inc.:* Ken M. Jones, 8; Marion
Patterson, 12; Jim Zipp, 16; Paolo Koch, 24; W.K. Fletcher, 26; George D. Lepp, 28; Bryan & Cherry Alexander,
41; Jacques Jangoux, 66, back cover; Herve Donnezan, 70. *Corbis:* Galen Rowell, 49; Frans Lanting, 53. *Tom
Warhol:* 51 (top), 51(middle), 51 (bottom).

Printed in China
1 3 5 6 4 2

CONTENTS

INTRODUCTION

TUNDRA, NOW AND THEN

A wide expanse of gently rolling terrain, with low-growing grasses, dwarf shrubs, mosses, and lichens, stretches for miles, seemingly without interruption. The plant life only seems to vary when the land is high enough to funnel the spring surface meltwater into a channel, or when water collects in a low-lying bog—this moisture allows different plants, like small trees and some wildflowers, to take root. Few sounds can be heard and no movement seen other than the howl of the wind and the grasses swaying to its rhythm.

Suddenly, a low rumble shatters the calm, and the ground begins to shake. What is it: an approaching thunderstorm? an earthquake? No, but something just as dramatic: the yearly migration of North America's barren-ground caribou. Numbering in the tens of thousands, the caribou herds travel hundreds of miles, migrating from their wintering grounds in the taiga, or boreal forest, to their summer calving grounds here in the tundra. The lichens and other plants provide caribou mothers with the proper nutrition to make rich milk for their newborn calves.

The whole herd will spend the summer in the north, sometimes alongside their feared enemies, wolves, without being attacked by them. In years of peak population growth, lemmings provide enough food

A caribou herd crosses the tundra in Alaska's National Wildlife Reserve.

for the wolves' summer diet. These are good times for the caribou. They are able to raise more calves, which are usually the easiest target for the canine predators.

This is the cycle of life here in the Arctic tundra. After months of quiet, with the land locked in the icy grip of winter, life bursts forth and races to take advantage of the precious days of plenty the summer provides.

The white-tailed ptarmigan, a grouse-like bird, prefers alpine habitats in Alaska and Canada where it feeds on willow and alder catkins in the winter, and leaves, flowers, and buds of various plants in the summer.

1

WHERE IS THE TUNDRA?

The harsh climate of Earth's tundra areas is what makes this biome unique. Tundra, originally a Finnish word meaning "barren and treeless land," is one of the simplest biomes. The plants and animals here have to make do with frigid winter temperatures; cool, short summers; and drought-like conditions, both because of the relatively small amount of precipitation that falls and because the long winters keep the life-giving water locked up in the soil as ice and snow, unusable by living things.

The diversity of life on Earth is greatest in the tropics, around 0 degrees latitude. Traveling north or south away from the equator reveals a gradually decreasing level of diversity until you reach the North and South Poles, at 90 degrees latitude, where nothing lives. The tundra biome consists of all lands above tree line—or the farthest extent to which trees can grow—and includes all lands up to the limit of plant growth, where snow and ice cover is permanent. Few species can live in these extremes.

There are two main types of tundra. Polar tundra, as the name suggests, lies close to the North and South Poles. The largest area of tundra is in the north, the Arctic. This includes parts of North America (Canada, and the United States), Greenland, Iceland, Scandinavia (Norway, Sweden, and Finland), and Eurasia (Siberian Russia and China). Polar tundra also exists near the South Pole in Antarctica.

Alpine tundra, the second type, lies on mountainsides and on high-elevation plateaus. (Elevation is the height above sea level.) Alpine tundra exists in many countries, even in tropical areas. It can be found in Canada and the United States (Rocky Mountains), Mexico (Sierra Madre), South America (Andean Mountains), Europe (the Alps, Pyrénées, and Carpathians), Africa (the Ruwenzori Mountains, Mt. Kenya, Mt. Kilimanjaro, the Lesotho Plateau), Asia (the Himalayan and Tibetan Plateaus), and New Zealand (North Island and Southern Alps).

Tundra Regions of the World

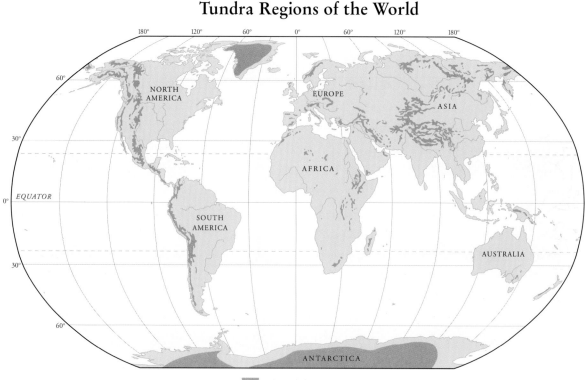

polar and alpine tundra

EVOLUTION

The tundra biome is among the youngest biomes on Earth. As recently as 65 million years ago, in the Paleocene epoch, tropical forest covered the lands that are now dominated by tundra vegetation. The climate cooled and warmed over long periods of time, and the vegetation changed with it.

Deciduous forests gradually replaced the tropical forests in the Oligocene epoch (23 to 36 million years ago). Coniferous forests became dominant as the climate cooled more, and mosses began to spread in the Pliocene epoch (2 to 5 million years ago).

The collision of continental and oceanic plates and subsequent volcanic activity pushed rock up and reformed it, creating mountains. For example, the New Zealand Alps were formed in the Pliocene epoch, while the Ruwenzori Mountains of Africa and the Andes Mountains of South America formed in the Eocene epoch (37 to 58 million years ago). Alpine vegetation colonized these high areas.

Many plants and animals were killed off by a series of widespread glaciations, or Ice Ages, that began in the Pleistocene epoch, around 2 million years ago. Huge sheets of ice, thousands of feet thick, formed at the poles and advanced over Earth as the climate cooled. In the interglacial periods—periods of warming between cold periods— the glaciers retreated, or melted.

Many species went extinct as a result of the Pleistocene glaciations. Afterward, the current plant and animal communities began to take shape. In the north, deciduous tree species like willow, aspen, and poplar hung on in moist, sheltered areas and developed more stunted forms as the climate became colder and harsher.

Life in Antarctica was subjected to even more intense cold, and many more plants and animals became extinct there than in the Arctic. Today, only remnants of tundra communities remain, mostly along the edges of this southernmost continent and on subantarctic islands.

Alpine tundra exists at its highest elevation in the Himalayan Mountains, which contain the highest peaks in the world.

Because they were above the level of the ice sheets, alpine areas were refuges for polar plants and animals when the glaciers were advancing. Many species adapted to these cold environments. Some even became new species in the process known as speciation. When the glaciers melted away, the plants and animals of the alpine areas were able to move into and colonize polar regions.

The alpine areas of the Himalayas are believed to be the source of many of today's plants and animals because of the rich diversity of creatures found there. During times of peak ice cover, the Bering Strait (the narrow body of water separating Alaska and Russia) was frozen over. This land bridge allowed the ancestors of large animals like bison, wapiti, and woolly mammoth to find their way from Asia to North America. Most of these creatures became extinct by 10,000 years ago due to another climate change.

Along the southern edges of the Arctic tundra, remnants of the taiga grow scattered among the grasses and shrubs, such as here in Denali National Park and Preserve in Alaska.

2

BARREN LANDS?

CLIMATE

The atmosphere interacting with the biosphere is what creates climate in a particular region. The rotation of Earth causes winds to move around the planet. These circulating high-pressure systems (cold air) and low-pressure systems (warm air) affect global temperature. They also affect ocean currents, moving cold and warm water from one region to another, moderating climate in polar regions by moving tropical waters to the north, for example. This is how climate becomes regulated on the planet.

The position of Earth relative to the Sun creates seasons, times of cold and warmth during the year. The seasonal change is not as great in tropical areas (near the equator) as it is in temperate or polar latitudes.

The cycle of sunlight in polar regions creates special challenges for life here. Because of Earth's tilted axis, these areas receive about six months of darkness and six months of sunlight, depending on the location. This means that most plant life goes quiet for the winter, but when the sun is out for twenty-four hours each day in the summer, life can be active, growing for that whole time.

The Arctic tundra can become flooded in summer when the upper layers of permafrost melt.

The lowest average annual temperatures and the lowest summer temperatures on Earth occur in the polar climates. Since daily temperatures do not rise into the proper range for plant growth until June, and winter takes hold as early as September, the main growing season only lasts for a maximum of about two months, two to three months less than in many temperate regions of the world.

Average monthly temperatures in the tundra regions are usually below the freezing point: 32 degrees Fahrenheit (0 °Celsius). During the summer, midday temperatures can rise to 70 °F (21 °C) in the Arctic. Winter temperatures can be as low as -71 °F (-7 °C), and frosts are possible even in the height of summer.

Most areas of the tundra receive very little precipitation, in some cases less than 5 inches (13 centimeters) a year. This moisture doesn't evaporate quickly because of the cold temperatures, and the permafrost layer below the surface prevents the soil moisture from draining away. So while plants and animals have to deal with drought-like conditions in winter, flooding can be a problem in summer, when the permafrost in the upper soil layer—known as the active layer—melts. But in most areas where there's not too much water, many plants take hold, and the active layer comes alive with soil organisms—nematode worms, spring-tails, and other soil invertebrates.

TREE LINE

There comes a point of latitude and altitude (elevation) where tree growth abruptly ends, called the tree line. At sea level, this usually occurs close to Earth's North and South Poles. As elevation increases, tree line can occur further away from the poles, to a maximum of about 13,000 feet (4,000 meters) on mountains in tropical areas. The trees at tree line tend to be evergreen—coniferous species near the poles and broadleaf evergreen species in the tropics.

Scientists often disagree about what cause trees to stop growing at high latitudes and elevations. Generally speaking, wind and intense sunlight seem to have the greatest effect. The dark color of foliage allows trees to absorb more heat from the sun in summer. Foliage temperatures can be as much as 25 to 30 °F (14 to 17 °C) higher than the surrounding air temperature in some alpine areas. This dries the foliage, often killing it.

High winds also have a strong effect on tree growth at tree line. The constant winds can dry leaves out quickly. Ice crystals carried along by the wind can destroy the fragile foliage and even wear the bark off trees. Some trees in alpine areas are able to adapt and avoid some of the worst effects of sun and wind. They do this by staying low to the ground, where temperatures are warmer and winds are less severe. Species of conifer such as black spruce take on a stunted growth form called krummholz (German for "crooked wood"), snaking along the ground and sending branches up only to a limited height.

Trees growing amid the tundra can be damaged by the strong winds and ice.

LIFE IN THE EXTREMES

There may not be a huge variety of plants and animals in the tundra, but the hardy organisms that do live here take hold and spread over large areas. Contrary to popular belief, temperatures in the boreal forest biome, south of the Arctic tundra, can actually be colder than in the tundra. Taiga plants and animals can handle the cold better than tundra creatures. More animals that live in the boreal forest hibernate than those that live in the tundra. Some plants in the boreal forest can withstand freezing temperatures even if they are not covered by an insulating layer of snow.

Plants

In polar tundra, low light levels during winter mean that plants, even evergreen ones, cannot photosynthesize at all. Although the sun is out all day even in spring and autumn, it stays so low on the horizon that the sunlight is not direct enough to provide much heat or energy. But during the peak of the summer, there's enough energy to allow plants to photosynthesize twenty-four hours a day. This gives plants the boost they need to stay alive. If the ground stays protected by the snow and doesn't freeze, some plants can begin to grow even before the snow melts in spring.

Tundra plants have to grow very quickly during this short period in order to get their business done. In many cases, their life cycles from flowers to seeds can't be completed in one summer season. The buds of some wildflowers may take as long as three summer seasons to form. Other plants have evolved only to grow by vegetative means; they send up new shoots from their roots and branches.

Another way plants in the tundra biomes, especially the polar regions, respond to the harsh climate is by staying small, not growing taller than 8 inches (20 cm). This low-growing habit helps protect plants from frost damage. Usually covered by winter snow, they stay insulated from the bitterly cold temperatures.

Because they need to stay under the snowpack in winter, some shrubs will grow horizontally along the ground, sending up many branches. Staying low also keeps them out of drying winds while they absorb as much sunlight as possible. Warmth and moisture build up and are held between their leaves and the ground, an important strategy in such a cold, dry environment.

Many of these plants have developed thick, leathery or waxy leaves that prevent moisture loss. Hairs along stems, leaves, and sometimes flowers hold heat and protect against wind. Some species grow in a cushion form, staying low and packed tightly together to hold heat and water. Leaves that are flat against the ground absorb the most sunlight possible.

Some plants grow with their leaves in a "rosette" form, a cluster of leaves enclosing a leaf bud. This growth form catches snow and dew, providing much-needed moisture while also protecting the bud from drying winds and freezing temperatures.

Many tundra plants are evergreen. Keeping their leaves for a number of years helps plants get a jump on growth in spring. If they don't have to pour out so much energy to create a whole new crop of leaves each year, like deciduous plants do, they can use that energy to grow and reproduce.

Animals

Animals of the tundra have adapted to the cold, dry conditions in a number of ways. The most common adaptation is to have a thick insulating layer of fur or feathers to hold the heat close to their bodies. Many large animals also have compact body shapes (wolverines and polar bears, for example), which helps them retain more heat than they would if they had long, thin bodies. Many animals can also build up a thick layer of fat quickly over the summer that keeps them warm and provides energy when food is scarce over the winter.

Another strategy is simply to avoid the cold by migrating. Many birds, caribou, and other animals make use of the tundra only in the productive summer months, spending the winter farther south in other biomes. Arctic terns do migrate, but they spend both summer and winter in polar lands. They nest along the coast of the Arctic Ocean during the Northern Hemisphere summer, then they fly south to take advantage of the plentiful sea life around Antarctica and the subantarctic islands during the Southern Hemisphere summer. This migration usually involves flying more than 20,000 miles (33,000 kilometers), the farthest any bird species is known to migrate.

Although hibernation seems to be an obvious method of dealing with the cold in this frigid habitat, female polar bears are the only tundra animals that hibernate. This is mostly because the short summer season sometimes isn't enough time for animals to build up the fat reserves they need to survive the long winter. Polar bears make their dens in snow caves. Other animals may burrow into the snow temporarily to escape harsh cold temperatures and winds. For rodents, the layer of permafrost prevents them from burrowing too far into the Earth. Hibernation as a cold-avoidance strategy occurs more commonly in boreal and temperate ecosystems.

Insects adapt to the cold in a number of curious ways. Some change their body chemistry, creating a natural antifreeze in their bodies. Cold-blooded creatures like reptiles and amphibians simply can't stay alive in the tundra biome. Over geologic time, as these regions have moved further north and become colder, these creatures gradually died out.

Despite these adaptations, however, winter is a long, hungry season, especially for the carnivorous mammals that stay active, like arctic foxes and wolves.

The tundra is the youngest biome on Earth. Most tundra landscapes have many lichen-covered rocks and areas of bare soil.

3

THE LAY OF THE LAND

GEOLOGY AND SOILS

The ground, the bedrock and soils, is where any ecosystem begins, and with tundra that beginning is so recent that you can see it written in the soil. Because of the nature of the climate, soil-forming processes happen very slowly here.

The thin soils of the tundra were the last areas to become free of ice when the glaciers retreated to their current position. These young soils are very nutrient-poor and acidic. In temperate regions, plant root growth, decomposition by bacteria and fungi, and the churning by soil animals keeps soils well mixed, allowing air and water to flow and plants to root even deeper. The soils of the tundra are frozen most of the year, so these organisms are active for a much shorter period of time. This keeps soils from becoming well developed.

Consequently, there are large areas of bare soil and rock, especially in the drier parts of the polar tundra and in the high alpine zones. Lichens and sometimes mosses are usually the only plants to colonize these areas.

The summer warmth only extends so far down into the soil. The upper layers of the soil that do melt and are alive with growth during the summer are known as the active layer. By the end of the growing period in August, this layer can reach from 20 inches (50 cm) in the northern parts of the Arctic tundra to 35 inches (90 cm) in the southern reaches. In some coarse, sandy, gravelly soil, the active layer can be as deep as 10 feet (3 m).

Many of the wetter areas of the tundra are actually covered by several feet of dead sphagnum moss. The temperatures are so low here that these plants can't decompose. Any creatures, animals or people, walking around these areas in summer would sink into the muck.

Flowing water and expanding ice beneath the permafrost feed the growth of pingos, hills of ice covered with soil and plants.

PERMAFROST

Permanently frozen ground, known as permafrost, lies beneath 26 percent of all the land on Earth and about half of all land in Canada and Russia. It can also be found in some alpine areas, as in the Himalayas. How far down this frozen soil goes depends on the local topography and climate. In some locations in Canada, permafrost may extends as far down as 2,145 feet (660 m). Scientists estimate that it took about 10,000 years for the ground to freeze so deeply.

Cyclical freezing, thawing, and refreezing can make the soil very unstable, and this affects the pattern of plant growth. As air temperatures drop below freezing, the ground begins to freeze, both from the sur-face downward and from the top of the permafrost layer upward. The unfrozen soil between these two frozen layer gets squeezed as pressure increases belowground. The soil is eventually forced up to the surface, resulting in soil boils. These show up as areas of bare loose soil and rocks. Plants have a hard time taking hold in this turbulent environment.

Because water expands as it freezes, the ground above it swells and expands. When this happens in wetlands, low mounds called palsas form. These permafrost mounds are about 3 feet (1 m) high and up to 98 feet (30 m) across. They're covered in peat, which are layers of dead plants, mostly moss, that builds up in wetlands.

In old lake beds, water draining in from surrounding areas feeds the growth of pingos, small hills that consist of soil and plants surrounding a core of ice. As long as the water flows toward it, these formations continue to grow. But if the ice within the hills melts, the ground will collapse. Roads, buildings, and other manmade structures have been damaged when the permafrost beneath them melted and collapsed.

When the permafrost beneath the tundra freezes or thaws, it may create patterns such as these polygons found in Canada.

PATTERNED GROUND

The yearly freezing and thawing of the active layer in tundra soils is more than just an inconvenience to plant growth. It is actually the primary shaper of the tundra landscape. The uneven, rolling terrain mixed with clefts and hollows forms a landscape of small streams and pools scattered across the landscape.

Aside from this general shape of the tundra terrain, the action of freezing and thawing of permafrost creates other, more unusual formations called patterned ground. There are many different shapes that form, including sorted and unsorted circles, polygons, stripes, and hummocks. The circles can be small, about 4 to 10 inches (10 to 25 cm) across, while the polygons range in size from 10 to 325 feet (3 m to 100 m).

Circles form in groups and are created when loose soil is forced aboveground by soil freezing belowground. The soil emerges and slowly forms a mound. In the sorted circles, stones that are forced out roll to the edges and collect there. This creates a circle of stones surrounding a mound of finer rocks and soil. Plants may take root along the edges where the soil is more stable, but while the center is active, plants cannot grow.

On slopes during the spring thaw, the soil above the top layer of permafrost becomes lubricated as it melts, and whole sheets of soil may slide downhill. This slow movement year after year can create a steplike pattern across a broad hillside. Plants may grow on the vertical riser of the steps, while the flat tread stays mostly bare because it is exposed to constant wind. Over time, the vegetated riser becomes buried as it slides downslope.

Polar bears move easily among sea ice, open ocean, and land in the Arctic.

4

LIFE AT THE TOP OF THE WORLD

The biomes of Earth are stacked somewhat like a layer cake. The tropical biomes are in the center layer, in a belt around the equator. Moving away from the equator in either direction, north or south, one will travel through the temperate biomes. Above this in the north, after passing through the large, continuous stretches of dense, coniferous tree growth of the boreal forest, one enters forest tundra, an ecotone between the two biomes. Only scattered smaller spruce and fir trees grow here amid a landscape of low-growing shrubs, wildflowers, mosses, and liverworts. Farther north lie the Arctic polar biomes—the open expanses of Arctic tundra and polar desert. Topping this off is the icing on the cake, the continuous snow and ice of the North Pole and the Arctic Ocean.

The Arctic region contains the largest areas of polar tundra in the world. North America has the most and Siberia is next. The Arctic can be divided into two regions, the High Arctic and the Low Arctic. Tundra occurs in the Low Arctic.

Arctic polar tundra is covered with snow for eight to ten months of the year. At the peak of winter, darkness exists for twenty-four hours a day, while in midsummer, the opposite—twenty-four hours of sunlight—occurs. The largest areas of permafrost exist here, as well as the best examples of patterned ground.

The topography of the Arctic is quite diverse, and this has promoted biological diversity in what would otherwise be fairly simple ecosystems. The landscape includes high mountains; flat expanses; low, rolling terrain; and large areas of exposed bedrock, such as the Precambrian Shield in central Canada.

PLANTS OF THE ARCTIC TUNDRA

The most common sight in the Arctic tundra is miles and miles of rolling grassland. The widespread grasses are the favorite food of caribou, muskox, and lesser snow geese during summer months. The cold, dry conditions of the Arctic tundra have favored plants that are small and can conserve heat and moisture well. Plants have evolved to grow only as tall as the snowpack allows.

There are about 600 species of plants that grow in the Arctic tundra, and many of these are common to all areas of northern tundra, from North America to Eurasia.

Most plants here are long-lived perennials, meaning their above-ground parts die back each year and sprout again from the same roots the next year. The short Arctic summers make it difficult for many plants to reproduce, so many plants branch out, growing new shoots from their branches and roots. Some plants do produce seeds, however, and these can stay viable in the soil for a long time until conditions are right to germinate. Seeds of a species of Arctic lupin that were buried under glacial soil for 10,000 years sprouted after they were found.

Most plants on the tundra remain relatively short, like these shrubs and grasses, a favorite food of the caribou and muskox.

The soils are so poor here that plants have had to develop other ways to get the nutrients they need. Bacteria living in the roots of some plants, called legumes, a plant family that includes the peanut, help the plants by absorbing nitrogen form the air. As they do this, the bacteria transform the gaseous nitrogen into nitrates, a form that plants can use for nutrition.

Other plants take advantage of patches of ground where animals congregate. Colonies of kittiwakes, a seabird on the Svalbard group of islands north of Scandinavia, leave behind large amounts of guano beneath their nests. Nothing can grow immediately below these cliff nests because the feces are so high in nitrogen. But the nitrogen becomes less concentrated as it leaches into the soil and nourishes nearby plant communities.

A dwarf willow plant has evolved to withstand the cold and snow of the polar tundra.

Plant Communities

Ecosystems all over the world are influenced and in some ways formed by the controlling effects of climate, topography, soil type, and other factors. The tundra plant communities are no different. In this biome, biodiversity decreases from the south to the north as the climate becomes gradually colder and drier. Most plant communities cover many square miles of the tundra.

Lichens and mosses are the most common plants in the tundra biome. They have just the right characteristics for survival here; they grow low to the ground and can withstand great changes in temperature and humidity. Huge areas of the High Arctic are covered by these plants almost exclusively, and they can be found growing amongst almost every other plant community as well. They help to stabilize the soil and provide places for other plants to grow.

The Arctic tundra can be broken down into five major plant communities based on location and soil moisture. The tallest shrubs and trees are found along streams, lakes, and on steep slopes where the active layer is deeper and there are more nutrients. Dwarf, shrubby willows, alders, and birches, from 6.5 to 16 feet (2 to 5 m) grow here. These plants grow as full-sized trees in the temperate biome. Many grasses and wildflowers grow beneath the trees.

Even smaller forms of these trees, from 16 to 23 inches (40 to 60 cm), grow on less-steep slopes and on upland areas just north of the forest tundra ecotone in Alaska and northwest Canada. Mosses, lichens, grasses, and shrubs fill in abundantly amidst the more scattered low canopy of willows and birches.

Dwarf shrubs 2 to 8 inches (5 to 20 cm) tall are found on low, rolling hills where soils have good drainage. Many of these species are heaths—shrubs with thick waxy leaves like blueberry, rhododendron, and Labrador tea—and can also be found in larger forms in biomes further south. These plants occupy smaller areas than other tundra communities. Sometimes cottongrass, a sedge with large white, puffy blooms, can be found growing with these plants.

On very wet ground, mosses and grasses grow together as a community. Since they can't absorb water like trees or wildflowers (vascular plants with an internal cell structure for transporting fluids), mosses tend to grow as tight mats or bundles. Water is absorbed through the surface of their leaves, and they can survive extreme drought.

Sedges and grasses often grow in tussocks, or mounds. By growing in a collective group, the sedges can create islands that stay above the water and hold the soil in place. Grasses on drier, windswept slopes are able to withstand the wind better when supported by each other in clumps. This tussock form also helps hold moisture and retain warmth.

On slopes blasted by cold, drying winds without much snow cover, a community of low-growing wildflowers mixed with lichens grows. These communities are more common in the High Arctic.

ANIMALS OF THE ARCTIC TUNDRA

Insects

Surprisingly, the Arctic tundra is richer than one would expect when it comes to insects and other soil invertebrates. The most obvious are the various fly species, like black flies and mosquitoes. During the short summer season, the abundant meltwater gives them plenty of places to lay their eggs. When they hatch, huge swarms blanket the tundra skies. But many insects, like some Arctic plants, need more than one summer to complete their life cycle.

Spiders are also common in tundra areas. In much of the Arctic, wolf spiders prowl the ground, hunting for insects and soil invertebrates.

Many insects stay alive during the winter by going dormant. They may produce a sort of antifreeze—glycerol and other chemical compounds—that lowers the freezing point of the water in their bodies. Their body temperatures can reach as low as -30 °F (-20 °C). Many have smaller bodies than their southern counterparts, and many are a darker color, enabling them to absorb more heat from sunlight than lighter-colored creatures can.

Mammals

Many tundra mammals—Arctic hare, ermine, lemming, and other species—change the color of their fur every year. During the snow-free summer, their fur is mostly brown. As the cold weather begins again in the autumn, these animals gradually shed their brown coat and grow a much lighter one that blends in better with the snow-covered winter landscape.

Since they blend into their environment, it is more difficult for predators, the animals who hunt them, to see and catch them. But this clever adaptation has also evolved in the Arctic fox, a predator that

The Arctic fox, seen here in its summer coat, feeds on a variety of foods, including lemmings, birds, eggs, insects, berries, and seaweed.

turns the tables by using this camouflage to sneak up on its prey.

Lemmings are one of the keystone species of the Arctic tundra. Their populations rise and fall drastically on a three-to-four-year cycle. This has serious consequences for the plants that they eat and the animals that eat them. In times of peak numbers, the lemmings may clear out grasslands of plants. However, these times are good for predators like snowy owls and Arctic foxes. Even caribou, normally herbivores, may eat lemmings when they are plentiful. But when the lemming populations crash, many predator populations also decline. Snowy owls fly south to find food; many never return and die of starvation.

During the summer months, lemmings dig burrows in the ground. This allows them to elude predators. In winter, they forage for plant roots in these burrows and ones they dig in the snow. Lemmings even mate and give birth during this time. While mostly protected by the

Many predators, including the Arctic fox and the snowy owl, rely on lemmings as a food source.

snowpack, these rodents may fall prey to weasels who discover their tunnels in the snow.

The Arctic hare and the Arctic fox are both active in winter. The hare feeds on plants in areas where the snow has been blown off by wind. The fox returns to caches of food stored during the summer—lemmings and birds' eggs, for example.

Only a few species of large mammals make the tundra their home. Moose only use the tundra occasionally when food in the coniferous forests becomes scarce. Muskoxen are true tundra animals, wandering in small herds of ten to twenty animals searching for grasses, lichens, and willow twigs. These large, stocky, horned animals weigh 500 to 800 pounds (227 to 363 kilograms) and have long fur coats in two layers.

Since they cannot outrun wolves when they are under attack, muskoxen will stand together in a line or circle and face their attackers in order to scare them off. While this strategy works well against wolves, it leaves easy pretty for human hunters. Muskoxen were hunted to extinction locally in Alaska in the mid-nineteenth century. A few dozen animals were brought from Greenland in the 1930s to repopulate the range. The new population has increased and is doing well.

There are several subspecies of caribou, or reindeer. Some live in forested habitats, but most use tundra for at least part of their life cycle. Woodland caribou, Peary caribou, and barren-ground caribou are found in the North American Arctic tundra, while the Svalbard reindeer is a smaller subspecies found on the group of islands off the northern coast of Norway.

Western woodland caribou spend winters in sheltered valleys in the Canadian Rocky Mountains and move above treeline to alpine tundra areas in summer. Peary caribou live farther north than the other two subspecies, spending all of their time in the northern islands of Canada. The Peary caribou is classified as endangered. These smaller caribou usually feed on grasses and lichen, which they dig through the snow to reach. Warmer winter temperatures have caused a cycle of freezing and thawing that leaves this food under ice, making it much harder for the caribou to dig.

Barren-ground caribou also eat mostly lichen during the lean winter months. The snow cover is usually thin or nonexistent in their winter range, blown off by the wind. But as with the Peary caribou, if these areas are ice-covered, many barren-ground caribou will starve. In spring, they gather in herds numbering in the tens of thousands and travel hundreds of miles north to their calving grounds, where the females give birth to their young.

To combat the cold, caribou have a coat of stiff, hollow hairs above a denser, wooly coat. Their wide, flat hooves help support them on hardened snow, while their long legs keep their bodies above the lighter snowpack.

Muskoxen, more closely related to sheep and goats than to oxen or cows, are known to the Inuit as omingmak, *which means "the animal with skin like a beard."*

Birds

The vast swarms of mosquitoes and black flies provide ample food for the many different birds that make use of the tundra in the summer months. The newly exposed wetlands are perfect habitat for the large numbers of waterfowl that breed here.

Other common bird species include jaegers, ptarmigans, loons, and geese. The dwarf shrub and cottongrass community provides good food and nesting sites for many different songbirds. Sandpipers, plovers, skuas, and seagulls use their long, narrow beaks to dig into the tundra for insects and other invertebrates. In Eurasian tundra, the Lapland bunting, snow bunting, and red-throated pipit are common.

Two species of ptarmigan, a grouse-like bird, spend the winter in the Arctic. The willow ptarmigan gets by on willow twigs, while the rock ptarmigan feeds on the catkins (male flowers) and buds of alder. When the weather gets especially cold and windy, they will bury themselves in the snow and wait it out. They have feathered feet with wide toes to make it easier to walk in the snow.

An arctic tern returns to its nest to feed its chick.

Polar Bears

Polar bears may be the most familiar of all tundra animals. These all-white bears evolved from their brown bear relatives about 150,000 years ago. They have adapted to their Arctic environment quite well. Polar bears have two layers of fur to keep them warm and a long muzzle for grabbing their main prey, ringed seals, through holes in sea ice.

Most bear species hibernate. They spend the winter in a dormant state in a den, cave, or hollow tree because there is usually not enough food to sustain them. When winter approaches, bears get ready by slowing down their bodily functions (heart rate, body temperature, waste recycling). This process takes weeks for most bear species.

Polar bears don't experience true hibernation but rather a state called walking hibernation. Their body temperatures do not drop as low as other bears', and they have the ability to switch quickly between this semi-hibernation state and an awake state. As a result, they can conserve energy during times when food is less plentiful, such as in the summer. This is usually a lean time for polar bears because the sea ice that provides a platform for their hunting has melted, making it harder to get to the seals.

Female bears dig their snow den in October. They settle in and give birth to one or two cubs two months later. Spring brings the mother and her cubs out of the den. The mother needs food badly at this point, as she has been nursing her cubs but hasn't eaten for almost nine months. Fortunately, the sea ice is still frozen, and seals also give birth at this time, so there is a lot of food for the bears.

Jaegers are known for their aggressiveness, especially when protecting their nests, as this long-tailed jaeger is doing against this Arctic wolf.

Ptarmigans change their coats like other animals in the tundra. But instead of two seasonal changes, they shed their feathers three times—in summer, fall, and winter. In summer, their feathers are brown, in winter, white, and their fall coat is a mix of white and brown—perfect cover among the patches of snow and bare ground.

Parasitic jaegers, gull-like seabirds that nest on the tundra, spend the winter at sea, following Arctic terns on their migration. The jaeger depends on the terns for food; it pirates food from them, sometimes chasing the terns until they drop the fish or other morsel.

PEOPLE OF THE ARCTIC TUNDRA

The harsh conditions have limited human settlement in the Arctic. Native peoples led lives of subsistence here, relying on land and sea animals for their food and other needs.

As with plants and animals, the native people of the tundra have their origins in Asia. Like many ancient mammals, they also likely used the Bering land bridge to cross over to North America. Many different groups exist throughout the Arctic, but the culture, language, and appearance of these different groups are similar. The commonly used term for these groups, Eskimos, was a name given to them by Europeans, and many natives consider it insulting. The different groups in Greenland and Canada refer to themselves collectively as Inuit, a word which simply means "people." There are also native peoples in Alaska and Siberia.

Many Inuit still live subsistence lives, hunting fish through the sea ice in winter.

The caribou and reindeer were once very important to the lives of Arctic peoples. They used as much of the animals as possible for their needs: meat for food, hides for clothing and shelter, and antlers and bones for tools. They also hunted the rich sea-based life—seals, whales, and fish.

Traditionally, the Inuit and other Arctic groups were nomadic, living in small groups and following food sources. Today, they have adopted a more modern lifestyle, staying in one place, working jobs, and using modern weaponry for hunting.

In 1999, the Inuit of Canada won their sovereignty from the government and established their own territory, which they named Nunavut. It was formerly part of the Northwest Territories. The Alaskan Inuit were granted land by the U.S. government in 1971 and now have their own businesses.

NATURAL RESOURCES

The discovery of oil and valuable minerals like coal and copper beneath the tundra stirred much interest in the Arctic. Modern technology made it easier for other cultures—among them American, Canadian, Russian—to explore and exploit the resources of tundra areas. Today, this exploitation, along with global climate change, is threatening elements of the Arctic tundra. Smelters, industrial plants that process minerals, have caused many problems in the Russian Arctic. And the American public remains bitterly divided over oil drilling in the Arctic National Wildlife Refuge.

When drilling is done in the winter, it has less impact than summertime drilling. The heavy machinery used to test and drill for oil compacts the active layer of soil, making it more difficult than usual for plants to gain a foothold in this harsh environment. Since the vegetation of the tundra regenerates so slowly, even minor disturbances can have a long-lasting effect. Eventually, these areas of disturbed tundra are transformed into marsh, as the soil is compacted and water rests closer to and on the surface. If an oil spill occurs, the shrubs and cottongrass on the upland tundra may take ten to twenty years to grow back after such an accident.

The pipelines constructed to carry the oil south from the North American Arctic into Canada and the United States are a barrier to some wildlife. Caribou and female moose and their calves steer clear of the areas around the pipeline and roads. This affects their migration and thus their survival. If they can't get to their calving grounds, they may not have enough to eat for the winter, so fewer will survive.

A cottongrass pond in Alaska's Denali National Park and Preserve.

Large animals of the Arctic have also been severely affected by hunting. Modern weapons have made it easier to kill creatures like wolves, caribou, and polar bears. These animals no longer exist in parts of their former ranges.

CONSERVATION

Although there has been significant damage to the Arctic tundra, people have begun to realize how fragile the landscape is, and some governments are doing something about it. Canada and the United States have set aside millions of acres as parks and refuges for wildlife and wilderness recreation. The first park in Alaska, Denali National Park, was set aside to ensure habitat for large mammals. Canada has five Arctic national parks of similar size. Iceland has established six nature reserves on the tundra. Northeastern Greenland National Park, at 240 million acres (97,128,000 hectares), is the largest Arctic reserve and the largest national park on Earth.

A grey-headed albatross protects its chick. Many albatrosses make their nests in grassy sections of the islands around Antarctica.

5

ANTARCTIC POLAR TUNDRA

Antarctica is the fifth-largest continent and covers 10 percent of Earth's surface. But contrary to popular belief, Antarctica is not all ice. It's just mostly ice.

As a matter of fact, the Antarctic ice cap contains 90 percent of the world's ice. The continent is so large that the cold air that it generates influences climate all over the world. Less than 5 percent of the continent has ice-free areas that are suitable for plants to grow. The subantarctic islands in the Southern Ocean foster a wider diversity of life.

A CONTINENT OF ICE

Climatic conditions in Antarctica are much more extreme than in the Arctic. The Antarctic continent is actually the highest, driest, windiest, and coldest continent on Earth. As in the Arctic, most of the solar radiation that hits Antarctica is reflected by the snow and ice. Only a small amount of the continent can absorb the Sun's heat, so the cold here is even more intense than in the Arctic

The average thickness of the ice cap is 7,963 feet (2,450 m), and the average elevation is about 7,443 feet (2,290 m), with some mountains as tall as 16,250 feet (5,000 m). There are some microorganisms—bacteria, yeasts, and algae—that live on the inland ice, but they are not part of the tundra communities.

Average January temperatures along the coasts are between 17 and 32 °F (-8 and 0 °C), while the inland may experience temperatures between 5 and 17 °F (-15 and -8 °C). In the west, on parts of the Antarctic Peninsula, the climate is more influenced by the ocean and thus is warmer and milder than the rest of the continent.

On mainland Antarctica, plants can only colonize coastal areas, where the Antarctic Ocean keeps the climate milder than the inland and the ground stays warm and free of ice. These areas, like the plant communities of the High Arctic, are considered polar deserts. Areas on north-facing slopes receive the most sunlight. This helps create better conditions for plant growth in this part of Antarctica.

Many islands near the continent and farther into the Southern Ocean are in the subantarctic zone, just outside the Antarctic zone. The smaller ones are no more than isolated rocks in the sea, but some islands and island groups, such as the South Orkney Islands, South Shetland Islands,

A colony of chinstrap penguins breeds on one of the South Shetland Islands.

and South Georgia Islands, are quite large and provide valuable breeding habitat for the Southern Ocean fauna. The plant communities on some of the islands surrounding the Antarctic continent are more properly called tundra communities.

LIFE AT THE BOTTOM OF THE WORLD

Antarctic Continent and Antarctic Peninsula

With the combination of harsh climate conditions and few sites without ice, the potential for life in Antarctica is very limited. Growth and decomposition are very slow processes here. There is little to no organic litter on the ground, so plants have to get their nutrients from rocks, the air, and wastes that wash in from the ocean or are left behind by breeding animals.

Ecologists have described only two main vegetation formations in this region—lichen and moss communities and grasslands. Grasslands grow along the northwestern part of the Antarctic Peninsula and nearby islands. The main continent has only various combinations of lichen communities.

The roughly 350 species of lichens grow on bare rock and soil alongside microorganisms such as cyanobacteria and microalgae. Mosses sometimes grow in these areas as well.

Other plant life has a hard time taking hold because these areas are constantly buffeted by winds coming from the inland ice cap and from cyclonic storms at sea. As a result, there are only two vascular plants that grow on the continent, Antarctic hair grass and Antarctic pearlwort. Both of these plants also grow on nearby islands.

Where conditions on the exposed rock and soil are exceptionally harsh, plants may only be able to grow inside porous and cracked rocks.

An Antarctic fur seal rests in tussock grass on South Georgia Island.

Subantarctic Islands

Plant and animal life are much more diverse in the subantarctic islands. The more hospitable, milder, and wetter climate allows flowering plants and more extensive grasslands to take hold and even allows bogs to form in wetter areas. Dense tussock grasses fringe the coastlines of these islands.

Long, narrow South Georgia Island lies about 1,250 miles (2,000 km) to the east of Tierra del Fuego, the tip of South America. Large mountain ranges run the length of the island, reaching to a maximum height of about 1,800 feet (2,900 m). The 25 percent of the island that stays free of ice and snow in summer provides nesting grounds for the largest concentration of wildlife in the world. Millions of penguins, fur seals, and seabirds return each year to crowd the shores of the island and raise their young. There are twenty-five species of vascular plants that grow on South Georgia and, along with a few hundred species of mosses, liverworts, and lichens, they form the basis for these island ecosystems.

On South Georgia Island, the tundra becomes free of snow and ice for the short summer.

Lichens

Lichens are organisms composed of two or more partners: a fungus and an alga. The resulting life-form may look almost nothing like the two partners. The alga photosynthesizes, producing food for both the fungus and the alga (the singular form of algae). What the alga gets from the fungus is protection from intense light, water and minerals that the fungus absorbs, and a special substance that speeds up photosynthesis. Of the approximately 25,000 known species, each lichen has its own particular fungus species associated with it, while only some algal species partner with the many different fungi.

The fungus part of the organism is what controls what the lichen looks like and what it does. Lichens grow in a variety of different ways, depending upon their environment and substrate (the surface on which they grow). Crustose lichens often grow in colorful patches imbedded in bare rock or on trees; foliose lichens are leafy in appearance and more loosely attached to the substrate; fruticose lichens assume a variety of forms, from hairlike to shrubby to fingerlike, and often hang from branches of trees and shrubs. Most lichens do not harm the plants they grow on.

Lichens are found in a wide range of habitats, from the tropics to the poles, and can tolerate all ranges of temperature, moisture, and soils. They can persist for centuries in extreme environments such as deserts, the Arctic, and on bare rock.

These pioneers are often the first organisms to colonize bare ground. Once established, they trap moisture and windblown soil, which, if conditions are right, allows other plants to take root.

Soil-inhabiting lichen can be important agents of stabilization in sand dunes, deserts, prairies, and alpine areas, reducing the effects of erosion.

Lichen species that colonize rock surfaces actually create soil. Their rhizines (root-like structures) penetrate the surface of the rock, straining the rock as they grow, expand, and contract with fluctuating moisture levels. The fragments of rock they dislodge become part of the soil. In this way, lichens are true pioneers.

Crustose lichen.

British soldier lichen.

Foliose lichen.

ANIMALS OF THE ANTARCTIC AND SUBANTARCTIC

Insects and Other Invertebrates

The Antarctic is unique in that the only land-based animals here are tiny invertebrates—soil organisms and insects. These include nematode worms, springtails, moths, spiders, and mites. One mite species is actually the southernmost animal in the world. They feed off organic wastes and windblown particles.

Mammals

One of the main differences between the Arctic tundra and the Antarctic tundra is that the few mammal species that do use the Antarctic continent don't feed on land; they get their meals in the sea. Seals only come onto land to breed, and most don't even make it to the continent but use the nearby subantarctic islands. The limited ice-free areas are densely crowded with these animals during the short summer season.

Fur seals, elephant seals, and others migrate north after the breeding season because the krill and fish they feed on, which stay close to the surface of the ocean during the summer, die off, migrate, or move to lower levels of the sea as winter approaches.

Birds

About fifty different seabird species breed in the Antarctic, but they spend the rest of the year at sea. Some of these species are shearwaters, fulmars, petrels, albatrosses, skuas, cormorants, and terns. Many of them gather in colonies millions or even tens of millions strong during the breeding season.

A subantarctic skua steals a penguin egg for food.

Wilson's storm petrels are migratory, traveling all the way from the North Atlantic to nest in Antarctica among the rocky terrain and even in tunnels they dig beneath rocks.

Although there are no land-based predators, petrels and other nesting birds need to watch out for fellow avians. Skuas will hang around the colonies of other seabirds, waiting for a nest to be left unprotected or scaring away the parents. They then grab the young and eat them.

Gulls and cormorants use lichens, mosses, and kelp to make their nests. Penguins pile up pebbles and stones. Emperor penguins are unusual in that they breed during the antarctic winter, huddling together for warmth on the sea ice at the edge of the continent.

ANTARCTICA AND PEOPLE

Because of the harsh climate and lack of significant plant and animal life, Antarctica does not support many people and no major cultures used this region. The world was not even aware that the continent existed until the mid-1800s.

There were rumors about a "southern land" before this, but not until the 1820s were ships plying the region, exploring the islands and the Antarctic Peninsula. The continent itself was discovered in the 1840s. The rich ocean waters surrounding the continent promoted intensive commercial exploitation, including sealing and whaling. Many marine species are still recovering. The lower numbers of whales due to over-fishing has resulted in increased numbers of penguins.

Exploration increased in the early twentieth century, and research stations began popping up after World War II. Today, there are twenty-seven manned stations on Antarctica from many different nations. Seven nations have made claims to some lands, but other nations do not recognize them.

The Antarctic Treaty, signed in 1959, provides protection for animals and plants and dictates that only scientific research is allowed on the continent. To be a treaty member, a nation must stake a claim, or set up a station or base. As a result, many governments have established bases there, mostly on coastal areas where the majority of life exists. This can cause major damage to Antarctic ecosystems.

Antarctica still faces many threats today. Commercial fishing has caused major waves in the marine ecosystem, which directly influences land-based life. With less fish and krill in the water, there is less waste material washing ashore, which means less food for bird and mammal species who rely on this waste for food.

Research and tourism have damaged the plant life and caused disruptions to penguin colonies. Noise, ogling humans, and air traffic scare penguins off their nests, leaving their eggs exposed to predators.

Scientists have discovered that pollution from countries all over the world seems to collect at the poles, causing damage to the ozone layer, the layer of the atmosphere that provides Earth with protection from harmful ultraviolet light. In 1997, the hole was estimated to be 10,424,754 square miles (27 million km^2), the largest ever recorded. One species of icefish has shown signs that changes are occuring in its DNA, and some one-celled plant life has also been damaged by radiation exposure through the ozone hole.

South Georgia Island was at one time a major whaling station, and about 2,000 people lived on the island, Today, the island is a United Kingdom territory with no permanent residents. Scientific researchers live there only part of the year.

A stream flows through a Polylepis *forest in the Andes Mountains.* Polylepis *trees thrive in some alpine tundra regions*

6

ALPINE TUNDRA

The polar regions are not the only place on Earth where expressions of the tundra biome can be found. Strangely enough, traveling in high mountain regions as far away as the tropics will bring a hiker into similar habitats called alpine tundra. The word "alpine" comes from a mountain range, the Alps, in Europe. Other mountain ranges in the world have the same name; there are also Alps in New Zealand for example.

When traveling up taller mountain in some parts of the world, a number of different ecosystems are usually encountered along the way. The change in climatic and soil conditions with elevation favors some species over others. In the Desert Southwest of the United States, as many as nine different ecosystems are expressed, from flat desert to the high-elevation alpine, with stops in shrub, forest, grassland, and various other zones on the way up. The alpine zone is usually the highest ecosystem on these mountains. The subalpine belt is the ecotone between the forested slopes and the alpine zone. Usually, a mix of tundra and evergreen forest grows here.

Alpine tundra is found in a band around the tops of mountains, usually between the tree line and rocky peaks, glaciers, or snow. Tundra occurs above 10,000 feet (3,000 m) on mountains near the equator and at progressively lower elevations farther away. Eighty percent of alpine areas are in the Northern Hemisphere.

Although many characteristics of alpine tundra—low precipitation, below-freezing temperatures—are similar to polar tundra, there are some basic differences, especially in tropical alpine zones. At higher latitudes, in temperate and near polar areas, many plants and animals are similar, but in alpine areas far away from the poles, very different and unusual plants grow. Patterned ground forms less extensively in alpine tundra, but stone stripes and nets do occur.

SUBARCTIC ALPINE TUNDRA

Alpine areas of arctic and subarctic climate can be found in the Scandinavian countries of Norway, Sweden, and Finland. While the northern parts of the region are relatively flat and more like polar tundra, much of the region is mountainous, especially western Norway.

Norway's long narrow shape and the large expanse of coastline in the west allows warmer air from the ocean to affect the climate there. But cold fronts that sweep down from the north limit this warming effect on the rest of the region. Being close to the North Pole also means that there is twenty-four hours of daylight for two months of the year.

The elevation of tree line in Scandinavia varies widely because of the varied topography. Tree line occurs at about 3,900 feet (1,200 m) in the mountains of Norway, at 1,300 to 1,625 feet (400 to 500 m) near the coast, and at sea level in very far northern Norway. Mountain birch is the main species forming tree line in Russia, Iceland, Greenland, and Scandinavia.

Taller shrubs and thickets of small trees, mostly willows mixed with birch and juniper and underlain by mosses and liverworts, mark the low

A tundra bog is surrounded by moss beds in the Norwegian Arctic.

alpine zone. These are mixed with short evergreen heaths, mostly made up of dwarf bilberry. Patches of evergreen grasses are also occasionally mixed in, but they are more widespread in the next highest zone, the midalpine belt. As in the High Arctic, the high alpine belt is sparsely vegetated with lichens and mosses scattered amongst the stones, and patterned ground is common.

The summer season brings swarms of mosquitoes and midges to the subarctic alpine zones. People and animals find these insects annoying and even painful, but they provide an invaluable food source for many songbirds and their young, raised on the tundra.

Many of the bird species of this region are the same as in polar tundra. Ptarmigan are common, year-round residents of grassland tundra. Bogs and mires in the low alpine zone support their own bird species, including many waterfowl, plovers, and snipe.

Aerial predators, including snowy owls, rough-legged hawks, golden eagles, gyrfalcons, and short-eared owls, feast when small mammals like lemmings are plentiful. Most of these raptors nest and perch on steep mountainsides, scanning for rodents in the low alpine growth.

The carnivorous mammals of the region are mostly forest animals who only sometimes use the tundra, such as brown bear and lynx. Wolves, nearly extinct in the region, hunt the reindeer who graze the tundra. Wolverines also prey on reindeer, especially in winter.

TEMPERATE ALPINE TUNDRA

Tundra in temperate and tropical regions exists only at high elevations. There are many mountain ranges in the temperate regions of the world that are tall enough to support tundra growth.

Around one-third of North America's Rocky Mountains lies above treeline, making conditions perfect for alpine tundra to occur, even in the southern part of the range, as in here in Colorado.

Gyrfalcons

The two species of ptarmigan, rock and willow, are the favorite food of the gyrfalcon, the largest of the falcons. Mostly gray, this falcon also may be seen in other color variations from white to blackish-brown. It lives year-round in the alpine areas of Scandinavia, and it can be found in many Arctic tundra regions as well.

This beautiful, efficient hunter scans for ptarmigan or lemmings from a rocky perch. When it spots one, the gyrfalcon dives into a low glide, hugging the ground only to rise up, then drop quickly onto its prey. This falcon will also chase until the prey is exhausted or sometimes even snatch ptarmigan from the air.

Gyrfalcons are not as common as they once were. In the past century, reindeer have become more numerous and have overgrazed the tundra vegetation. This has caused the rodent and ptarmigan populations to drop because they have less grass for food and cover from predators. As a result of this reduction of their food source, as well as human disturbance to their habitat, gyrfalcon numbers have dropped.

Some of the youngest mountain ranges in the world are in the long chain stretching from the Alps of western Europe all the way into Asia. Alpine tundra grows at its highest point in the central Himalayas, where tree line ends at 13,000 feet (4,000 m). This is the most southerly expression of the alpine biome in the Northern Hemisphere.

Many mountainous regions cover China and the former USSR, including the Carpthians, Altai, Sayan, and Tarbagatay mountains, which all lie within the deciduous forest zone. The Tien Shan range lies within the desert zone.

North American expressions of temperate alpine tundra occur most notably in the Rocky Mountains, which extend north to south from Canada well into the United States. Smaller, areas also occur in the eastern United States, for example, in the White Mountains of New Hampshire.

Temperate alpine tundra occurs in the Southern Hemisphere in New Zealand and in the Kingdom of Lesotho in southern Africa.

European Alps

The broken central and southern European mountain chain that includes the Alps, Pyrénées, Carpathians, Balkans, and Caucasus mountain ranges is one of the youngest mountain systems in the world. Many of these mountains contain glaciers and large areas of alpine tundra. They are the first mountain ranges south of the North Pole to differ significantly from polar tundra.

The mountain range known as the Alps extends for 750 miles (1,200 km) through France, Germany, Switzerland, Italy, and Austria. One of the best-known and tallest mountains is 15,771-foot (4,807-m) Mont Blanc in France.

This expression of alpine tundra lies between the deciduous forests and Mediterranean chaparral of Europe. Alpine tundra forms at elevations up to 9,750 feet (3,000 m) in the east and up to 13,000 feet (4,000 m) in the west. Since the regional climate is relatively warm for tundra, permafrost does not form.

The lower alpine zone favors dwarf shrubs, while the high alpine zone supports grasslands. Plants have a hard time gaining a foothold in areas known as screes, steep slopes where loose gravel slides downhill.

New Zealand Alps

The North and South Islands of New Zealand lie in the southwest Pacific Ocean, just southeast of Australia. North Island has smaller mountain ranges scattered mostly along the south part of the island. The Southern Alps extend all the way down long, narrow South Island, close to the western coast.

The New Zealand mountains are even younger than the European Alps, having formed in the Pliocene (5 to 2 million years BCE). They are still active, as the Australian and Pacific tectonic plates move to-gether beneath the islands. Glaciers cap some of the higher mountains.

The climate tends to be humid, especially on the western side of the mountains, which catch much of the rain, causing a rain shadow on the eastern slopes. Although frost may occur during any month of the year, winters are not very cold, and temperatures generally stay warm enough to prevent permafrost from forming.

At tree line, beech trees take on the krummholz form, weighed down by wind and winter snows. Above this, tall evergreen grasslands cover the low alpine zone. Bogs form in wet areas, creating places for a wider diversity of species.

The high alpine zone is covered by shorter growth of smaller grasses, wildflowers, and dwarf shrubs growing more sparsely among rocky areas. Plants are able to root in soil-filled cracks in the rock. On slopes with scree, few plants can hang on. Spring snowmelt and rains make the rock even looser than normal.

Cushion plants also grow in communities similar to polar tundra. The constant winds cause these plants to migrate downwind. Their roots and aboveground parts grow away from the wind direction in a crescent shape.

A wide variety of insects call the New Zealand alpine tundra home, including moths, beetles, flies, grasshoppers, and cicadas. Spiders are also common, including wolf spiders and vagabond spiders. Many of these spend the winter beneath the snow.

Many species of birds use the alpine zone, including the New Zealand falcon and the Australasian harrier, which soars over the grasslands, hunting rodents. But the only bird species that spends the whole year in the alpine zone is the rare rock wren. As the name suggests, this small bird nests and even spends the winter in rock crevices.

New Zealand also hosts the world's only known alpine parrot, the kea. This smart bird is noisy and curious, swooping down on hikers and investigating their gear. The myth that they are sheep killers has caused them to be persecuted by ranchers and turned them into an endangered species.

The mountains of New Zealand are the home of keas, the world's only alpine parrots. These smart and inquisitive birds find food in many different places, such as this bird rooting around stones for insects.

TROPICAL AND SUBTROPICAL ALPINE TUNDRA

The harsh climate of tundra regions makes for much less diverse ecosystems than that of tropical rainforests or even boreal forests. That said, alpine tundra in the tropics and subtropics is more biologically diverse than any other alpine tundra region.

The tropical climate and abundant broadleaf evergreen vegetation below tree line creates and holds humidity, which provides a steady supply of moisture for alpine plants.

Instead of big annual fluctuations in temperature, as in arctic tundra, tropical alpine areas show wide daily fluctuations. Nighttime temperatures often reach below the freezing mark while the days can be hot. This pattern is consistent year-round.

Since the amount of sunlight varies so little during the year, there are no seasons as there are in temperate and polar regions. As a result, permafrost doesn't form here. Despite the higher humidity, the large wetlands that are typical of Arctic tundra do not form because the soils are thin and don't hold water as well.

South America

The Andes Mountains, which extend 5,500 miles (8,900 km) along the western border of South America, support extensive areas of alpine tundra. The Northern Andes—in parts of Venezuela, Colombia, Ecuador, and Peru—contain *páramos,* which are cold, humid formations of grasslands and shrublands. Many Andean rivers begin in the páramos. *Puna* are similar formations in the Southern Andes (Peru, Bolivia, Argentina, and Chile). This type of alpine tundra is drier than the páramos and contains grasslands with scattered dwarf shrubs and trees.

The páramos, like other alpine tundra areas, are surrounded by forests at lower elevations. These mountaintop tundras have become

Frailejons, seen here growing in the tropical alpine tundra of Ecuador, are members of the daisy family and produce large, sunflower-like flowers.

islands in the sky, isolated from other alpine zones. This makes it difficult for seeds and animals to move between patches of alpine tundra.

Páramos vegetation today consists largely of small plants. However, some rosette plants called *frailejons* can grow to heights of 15 feet (4.5 m). As their leaves die, they don't fall to the ground but stay attached and form a protective cover for the thick trunks, insulating them from the cold, heat, and wind. The dead leaves also provide a home for many animals, from insects to mice and birds.

Grasses which grow densely among the frailejons, help to hold the soil in place. The grasses also provide food for many animals. Mosses are common here, and even orchids can be found at these elevations. Above 13,650 feet (4,200 m) little or no plant growth occurs.

Páramos plant communities are partly shaped by rabbits and deer as they eat the grasses and wildflowers. Some plants contain chemicals that make them undesirable, so these species are left behind in favor of the tastier ones.

One of the largest plants in the páramos and puna, the *coloradito* or *Polylepis,* forms small stands of dense forests. Recent research has confirmed that the Andean highlands were once covered by these forests. Researchers suggest that the current plant communities came about due to human-caused fires and livestock grazing. Seedlings of this now rare plant only grow in locations inaccessible to cattle and sheep.

Polylepis woodlands are important for many creatures, including numerous threatened bird species. These areas have richer soil and support more species of plants and animals than any other Andean community. Reforestation efforts are underway, but local governments have planted many nonnative tree species instead of *Polylepis* because they grow much more quickly and provide more income from harvesting than the slow-growing *Polylepis.*

Africa

Formed 35 million years ago by the separation of two tectonic plates, the Great Rift Valley in central and eastern Africa runs 3,100 miles (5,000 km), from northern Syria to Mozambique. The friction and pressure of this separation formed a number of volcanic mountains alongside the rift. Many of these stand alone, including Mt. Kilimanjaro and Mt. Kenya, on the east side of the rift, while the Ruwenzori range, a chain of mountains, lines the western side. To the north, more than ten mountain areas in Ethiopia make up a large highland plateau more than 13,000 feet (4,000 m) high. These include the Bale Mountains and the Simien Mountains.

The alpine tundra of these mountains, known as the afroalpine zone, supports similar plant communities to the South American páramos. Low-growing forms of heath shrubs, grasses, rosette and cushion plants are common.

Giant groundsels are one of the most unusual plants in the afroalpine zone of the Eastern African mountains. These plants grow up to 10 feet (3 m) tall and are similar to the frailejons of the Andes. The leaf rosettes resemble artichokes and close at night to protect the bud at their center from freezing. Their stems are protected from cold and wind by dead leaves.

Some of the mammals that use the afroalpine zone include the Walia ibex, a member of the goat family, and the mountain nyala, a type of antelope. The gelada baboon spends its time feeding in the grasslands of the afroalpine zone in the Bale Mountains. Its fingers are specially adapted to sort through grass and dig for roots of grasses. All of these

Gelada baboons live in groups of up to 400 individuals in the alpine zones of Ethiopian mountains. They feed on grasses, roots, and seeds in alpine meadows by day and sleep on nearby cliff ledges at night.

An endangered Ethiopian wolf crosses a patch of grassland in Ethiopia's Bale Mountains National Park.

mammals are endemic to the Ethiopian highlands, meaning they live nowhere else. The Bale Mountains in Ethiopia have more endemic mammals than anywhere else in the world.

Many unique species of spiders and beetles inhabit the afroalpine zone. To escape freezing nighttime temperatures, they seek shelter in the burrows of giant mole rats. The giant mole rat is the main food for the Ethiopian wolf, perhaps the only wolf species to inhabit an alpine zone. This species lives only in the highlands of Ethiopia and is considered by some to be the rarest mammal in the world. It is threatened by hunting, habitat destruction, and competition and interbreeding with the domestic dog.

The Ethiopian wolf shares the rodent population with three large raptors, the Augur buzzard, Mackinder's eagle owl, and Verreaux's eagle. A rich variety of birds makes use of the afroalpine zone, including sunbirds (similar to hummingbirds), swifts, chats, and snipes.

HUMAN USE OF ALPINE TUNDRA

Alpine areas, while not settled heavily because of the harsh climate, have been important historically for many cultures. Alpine tundra has mostly been used for summertime grazing of cattle and growing of grain.

Some permanent settlements near tree line in the European Alps served as bases for sheep raisers. Even steep slopes were planted with hay for animal feed. This practice increased the instability of the mountain sides, making them even more prone to landslides and avalanches. Many of the settlements were abandoned after the second world war, but alpine farming still occurs in Switzerland, Germany, and Austria.

Ancient peoples used the mountainous areas of Scandinavia for centuries, up until the Middle Ages. This mostly ended when people began to farm and raise livestock in the lowlands. Today, nomadic Laplanders still herd

Laplanders, people of the northern Scandinavian mountains, still raise reindeer, grazing them in alpine grasslands and tundra.

reindeer in the northern parts of the region, moving their herds from coastal areas in the summer to inland pastures in the winter.

Over the centuries in Iceland and in the Himalayas, livestock have probably grazed every inch of the alpine meadows. In the European Alps, the natural tree line no longer exists; clearing to create pastures for grazing has forced it lower. In tropical Africa, alpine areas receive much more rain than the hot, dry lowlands do, making the alpine zone and adjacent forests much more appealing for agriculture.

The Andean páramos and puna are used extensively for farming, including growing grasses and potatoes. Grazing by cattle is causing major changes to the vegetation as well, especially when humans burn land to create more pasture. Reforestation with pine and eucalyptus plantations reduces the diversity of these unique high-elevation communities. Some national parks have been established in order to protect the areas' water sources, the lagoons that serve as headwaters for many rivers in the high Andes.

Increasing in tourism in alpine areas has also caused damage to the fragile ecosystems. Construction of ski slopes has caused severe damage to the soil and vegetation and even altered local climate. In the European Alps alone, about 49,400 acres (20,000 ha) of these lands have been converted to ski runs.

CONCLUSION

TUNDRA AND GLOBAL CLIMATE CHANGE

Every day, climate researchers are finding more and more evidence that the Earth is warming. Unusual weather patterns are causing long-term droughts in some parts of the world and major flooding in others.

Scientists speculate and argue over the possible future effects of a rise in global temperatures. How much of this warming is normal variation, and how much is the result of human industry and alteration of the environment? If significant warming does occur, some say that the polar ice caps may melt, causing sea levels to rise and coastal areas to flood. Portions of the Antarctic Ice Shelf have already broken off from the main ice cap. This melting may also drastically alter the global circulation of ocean currents, changing the way warm and cold water moves around the planet.

One place that has received a lot of climate scientists' attention is the Arctic, where the effects of increased temperatures over the last century are already having major effects on ecosystems. Researchers in Alaska have shown that the last twenty years of the twentieth century, the average temperature of the active layer increased enough to melt the permafrost in some places. The southernmost

72

permafrost limit in China appears to be moving northward at a rate of 3 feet (1 meter) per year; similar changes are being recorded in Mongolia, Russia, and Canada.

Warmer temperatures bring deeper snows, which add to the overall warming by insulating the ground from subzero temperatures for a longer portion of each year, preventing freezing of the permafrost. The ice of permafrost holds the soil together. When the permafrost melts, the ground can collapse, destroying not only plant communities but also roads and houses.

Other ecological consequences of permafrost melting are that forests may begin to invade the tundra. Forests that now grow over tundra could turn into swamps, killing the trees. And one of the most frightening results that scientists envision could be that melting itself could add to global warming. Frozen tundra holds enormous amounts of carbon in its soils. When it warms up, bacteria, fungi, and other microorganisms become very active, decomposing the formerly frozen, dead organic matter. This activity releases carbon dioxide (CO_2), the main greenhouse gas that holds heat in the atmosphere. More melting may mean more heat, which means more melting and then more heat, and so on.

Warming may also raise the level of tree line in alpine environments, causing alpine species to be crowded out. With no similar habitat nearby to move or seed to, many species of animals and plants may become extinct.

Whether or not humans are at fault is immaterial to the effects of global climate change. But our efforts to reduce emissions of CO_2 into the atmosphere can still help the situation. Some governments have signed agreements to reduce their emissions of greenhouse gases. But many poorer nations may not be able to afford the changes necessary to reduce emissions. These countries are trapped between the choice of providing for their people and protecting the environment. Only by working together can many individual nations have an impact on global climate change.

GLOSSARY

biodiversity—The collective biological components of an ecosystem, including soil organisms, fungi, wildflowers, trees, insects, reptiles, amphibians, birds, and mammals.

carnivorous—Meat-eating.

ecotone—A transition zone between two biomes; species of both biomes may exist side by side in an ecotone.

germinate—To sprout or begin to grow.

global climate change—The process by which heat is trapped in the atmos phere by the buildup of carbon dioxide and other gases, raising the average global temperature.

guano—The feces of seabirds and bats.

keystone species—An organism that supports an ecosystem; fluctuating numbers of these species have an effect on many other other species in the ecosystem

legumes—A member of the pea family; these plants do not obtain nitro gen from the soil as most plants do, but receive nitrogen from bacteria in their roots that convert atmospheric nitrogen into nitrates for the plant's use.

permafrost—Permanently frozen ground; usually found well below the soil surface in tundra and some alpine ecosystems.

photosynthesis—The process whereby trees and other plants absorb sunlight, water, and carbon dioxide and convert them into carbohydrates (sugars) needed for plant growth.

rain shadow—An area, usually the side of a mountain facing away from the prevailing wind, where little precipitation falls.

topography—The shape of the land; for example, rolling hills, moun tains, or valley floors.

tussock—A mound or clump of grass.

viable—Being able to live and grow.

FIND OUT MORE

Books

Ruth, Maria Mudd. *The Tundra.* New York: Benchmark Books, 2000.

Tocci, Salvatore. *Alpine Tundra: Life on the Tallest Mountain.* New York: Franklin Watts, 2005.

Winner, Cheri. *Life in the Tundra.* Minneapolis, MN: Lerner Publications, 2003.

Web Sites

http://www.cotf.edu/ete/modules/msese/earthsysflr/tundra.html
This site was created by the Center for Educational Technologies at Wheeling Jesuit University. It also provides good information on biomes, diversity, adaptation, plate tectonics, and geologic time.

http://www.worldwildlife.org/ecoregions/index.htm
Finely detailed descriptions of world ecoregions devised by the World Wildlife Fund.

http://www.blueplanetbiomes.org
Descriptions of the world's Biomes by the West Tisbury School's sixth grade class in West Tisbury, Massachusetts.

BIBLIOGRAPHY

Angier, Natalie. "Built for the Arctic: A Species' Splendid Adaptations." *The New York Times*. January 27, 2004.

Barbour, Michael G., and William Dwight Billings, eds. *North American Terrestrial Vegetation.* United Kingdom: Cambridge University Press, 2000.

Cloudsley-Thompson, J. L. *Terrestrial Environments.* New York: John Wiley and Sons, Inc. 1975.

Historica Foundation of Canada. *The Canadian Encyclopedia.* 2004. http://www.canadianencyclopedia.ca/index.cfm?PgNm=Homepage&Params=A1

Kessler, Michael. "Forgotten Forest of the High Andes." Plant Talk On-Line, October 1998. http://www.plant-talk.org/Pages/15andes.html

The North American Outdoors. "Alaska-Yukon Barren Ground Caribou." 2003. http://www.naoutdoors.com/

Petersen, Wayne R. "Birds of the Long Sea Voyage." Sanctuary, Autumn 2003, pp. 3-5.

Marchand, Peter J. *North Woods.* Boston: Appalachian Mountain Club. 1987.

Natural Environment Research Council, British Antarctic Survey. 2004. http://www.antarctica.ac.uk/

Paulson, Dennis. "Biomes of the World." Tacoma, WA: University of Puget Sound, 1997. http://www.ups.edu/biology/museum/worldbiomes.html

Project Atlantis. South Georgia Island. 2004. http://www.sgisland.org/pages/sghome.htm

Revkin, Andrew C. "Alaska Thaws, Complicating the Hunt For Oil."
   The New York Times, January 13, 2004.

Revkin, Andrew C. "Unfrozen North May Face a Navy Blue Future."
   The New York Times. January 13, 2004.

Smith, Tim, John Coady, and Randy Kacyon. "Muskox." Alaska Department of Fish and
   Game, 1994. http://www.adfg.state.ak.us/pubs/notebook/biggame/muskoxen.php

Tarry, Emmalee. New England Seabirds and Pelagic Birding. 2000.
   http://www.neseabirds.com/index.htm

U.S. Central Intelligence Agency. The World Factbook. 2003
   http://www.cia.gov/cia/publications/factbook/index.html

Wielgolaski, F. E., ed. *Ecosystems of the World, Volume 3: Polar and Alpine Tundra.*
   Amsterdam: Elsevier Science B.V. 1997.

Woodward, Susan L. "Introduction to Biomes." Radford, VA: Radford University
   Geography Department, 1996.
   http://www.runet.edu/~swoodwar/CLASSES/GEOG235/biomes/intro.html

Wuethrich, Bernice. "When Permafrost Isn't." Smithsonian, February 2000.
   http://www.smithsonianmag.si.edu/smithsonian/issues00/feb00/phenom_feb00.html

INDEX

Tom Warhol is a photographer, writer, and naturalist from Massachusetts, where he lives with his wife, their dog, and two cats. Tom holds both a BFA in photography and an MS in forest ecology. Tom has worked for conservation groups such as The Nature Conservancy, managing nature preservers, and The American Chestnut Foundation, helping to grow blight-resistant American chestnut trees. He currently works for the Massachusetts Riverways Program, helping to care for sick, injured, and resident hawks, eagles, and owls. In addition to the Earth's Biomes series, Tom has authored books for Marshall Cavendish Benchmark's AnimalWays series, including *Hawks* and *Eagles.* He also writes for newspapers such as the *Boston Globe.* His landscape, nature, and wildlife photographs can be seen in exhibitions, in publications, and on his Web site, www.tomwarhol.com.